How to Draw
Everything
The Ultimate Guide for beginners

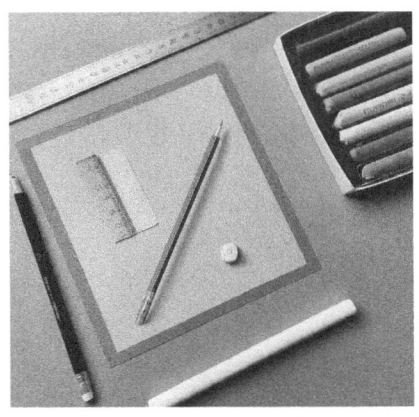

Harrison Simon

All rights reserved

No part of this book may be reproduced, distributed, or transmitted in any form or by any means, including; photocopying, recording, or other electronic or mechanical methods, without the prior written permission of the publisher, except in the case of brief quotations embodied in critical reviews and certain other noncommercial uses permitted by copyright law.

Harrison Simon

Table of contents

Introduction 8

Chapter One 10
   How drawing can help improve child concentration 10

Chapter Two 14
   How can parents support their child's interest in drawing? 14

Chapter Three 19
   At What Age Is Suitable to Introduce Drawing to Children? 19

Chapter Four 23
   Drawing can be highly therapeutic for children dealing with emotions due to several reasons ... 23

Chapter Five 27
   How can children overcome perfectionism in their artwork 27

Chapter Six 31
   Getting Started with Simple Shapes. 31
   Understanding Basic Shapes 35
   Tools and Materials Needed 37

Chapter Seven 43
   Exploring Shapes and Structures 43

Drawing Circles and Ovals................................45
Square and Rectangle.................................. 48
Draw triangles and polygons:..........................50
Chapter Eight.. 52
Transforming shape into object.......................52
Basic Object Drawing Exercises.................... 54
Combining Shapes Creatively.........................58
Adding Depth and Perspective......62
Chapter Nine..65
Adding Details and Texture............................ 65
Methods for adding subtleties........................ 67
Fun Shedding and Cross-Bringing Tips.......... 69

Chapter Ten... 70
Understanding Proportions and Scale............ 71
Scales and Measuring Items Accurately..........75
Tips for Maintaining Proportions..................... 79

Chapter Eleven..81
Mastering Lines and Curves........................... 81
Types of Lines and Curves and Their uses....85
Drawing Curves and Contour.........................89
Practice Line variation.....................................91

Chapter Twelve..93
Exploring Colors and Pattern.......................... 93
Basic Colour Mixing Technique for kids to know 96
Incorporating Pattern into drawing.................. 98

Chapter Thirteen 100
　Experimenting with Different Styles.............. 100
　Cartooning for Beginners............................. 103
　Realistic Drawing Techniques...................... 109

Chapter Fourteen 111
　Fostering your own style for youngsters' drawing... 111
　Finding Motivation for Kids Drawing.............115
Conclusion..118

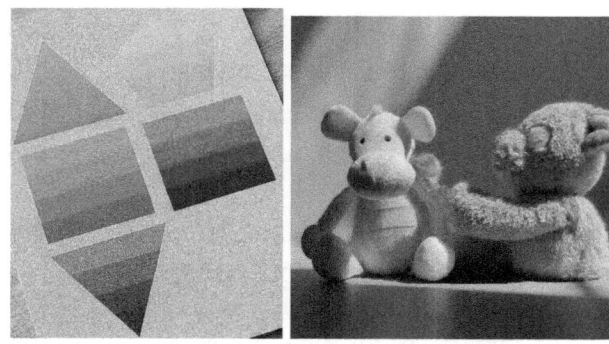
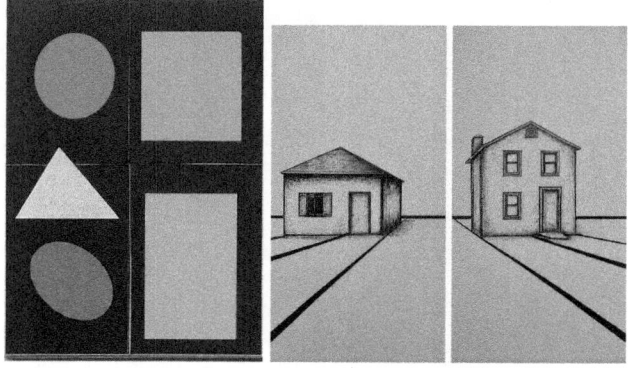

Introduction

Drawing is a magnificent type of articulation that permits youngsters to investigate their inventiveness and foster significant abilities. In this book, we will dig into the universe of drawing explicitly custom-made for youngsters. From basic shapes to adding mind boggling subtleties, we'll cover all that your kid has to be aware of to turn into a sprouting craftsman. Drawing isn't simply a great action; it likewise assumes a significant part in a kid's turn of events. It further develops dexterity, fine coordinated abilities, and fixation. Besides, drawing cultivates innovativeness and self-articulation, permitting kids to openly investigate their creative mind.

The underpinning of drawing frequently starts with basic shapes like circles, squares, triangles, and square shapes. These shapes act as building blocks for making more perplexing items. When youngsters know the fundamental shapes, they can figure out how to join them to address objects they find in their environmental elements. For instance, a circle can turn into a ball, a square can change into a house, and a triangle can be molded into a tree. Surfaces add profundity and authenticity to drawings. Kids can investigate various surfaces, like harsh, smooth, uneven, and fuzzy, to upgrade their work of art. Specifying includes focusing on little components that make a book interesting. Procedures like overshadowing, cross-bring forth, and texturing can be utilized to add profundity and aspect to drawings. Understanding the variety wheel assists youngsters with finding out about essential, auxiliary, and tertiary tones. It likewise shows them as reciprocal and practically equivalent to variety plans. By trying different things with variety blending, children can make a huge range of tones and shades. Blending essential varieties like red, blue, and yellow can deliver optional tones like purple, green, and orange. Cartooning includes drawing complex subjects into overstated, frequently comical drawings. It permits kids to foster their own novel style and characters. For those keen on catching the world as it shows up, sensible drawing strategies show kids how to precisely notice and reproduce objects.

Chapter One

How drawing can help improve child concentration

Drawing isn't simply a pleasant action for kids; it's likewise an amazing asset for upgrading their fixation and mental turn of events. In the present high speed world loaded with interruptions, assisting youngsters with building solid fixation abilities is fundamental for their scholastic achievement and by and large prosperity.

Stimulating Creativity Through Drawing

Drawing releases a kid's inventiveness and creative mind. At the point when youngsters participate in drawing, they have the opportunity to articulate their thoughts without limits. This innovative approach urges them to concentrate their contemplations and thoughts, prompting further developed focus levels.

Developing Fine Motor Skills

Drawing requires exact hand development and coordination, which assists youngsters with fostering their finely coordinated abilities. As they hold the pencil, control their developments, and control shapes and lines on paper, they are refining their coordinated movements, prompting better focus and dexterity.

Encouraging Focus and Attention to Detail

At the point when kids draw, they should focus on detail, like the shape, size, and position of items on the paper. This scrupulousness prepares their psyches to zero in on unambiguous assignments for expanded periods, further developing their fixation abilities over the long run.

Drawing as a Form of Relaxation and Stress Reduction

Drawing has remedial advantages and can help youngsters unwind and lessen pressure. Taking part in imaginative exercises like attracting permits kids to escape from regular tensions and spotlight their brains on the current second, advancing a feeling of serenity and inward harmony.

Incorporating Drawing into Daily Routines

Coordinating with day-to-day schedules can assist kids with fostering a propensity for concentrating. Whether it's devoting a couple of moments every day to bring before sleep time or integrating bringing exercises into self-teaching educational plans, creating drawing a standard piece of their routine can yield huge advantages for fixation.

Techniques to Promote Concentration While Drawing

Guardians and teachers can utilize different methods to assist kids with remaining on track while drawing. Empowering them to begin with basic representations and step-by-step progress to additional mind boggling drawings can forestall dissatisfaction and keep up with their advantage and focus levels.

Setting Achievable Goals for Drawing Activities

Defining feasible objectives for drawing exercises can persuade youngsters to accumulate and continue in their endeavors. Whether it's finishing a drawing inside a particular time span or dominating another drawing procedure, defining practical objectives assists youngsters with remaining on track and focused on their undertakings.

Drawing as a Device for Critical Thinking

Attracting urges kids to think basically and issue-solve as they make an interpretation of their thoughts into visual portrayals. When confronted with difficulties or slip-ups while drawing, kids figure out how to adjust, drive forward, and track down effective fixes, fortifying their fixation and mental abilities simultaneously.

Balancing Screen Time with Drawing Time

In the present computerized age, it's urgent to work out some kind of harmony between screen time and active exercises like drawing. Restricting screen time and empowering kids to take part in drawing exercises advances focus and decreases the unsafe impacts of exorbitant screen openness on their mental turn of events.

Encouraging Parental Involvement and Support

Guardians assume an essential part in supporting their kids' fixation abilities through drawing. Offering commendation and consolation, giving productive criticism, and effectively partaking in drawing exercises with their youngsters reinforces the parent-kid bond and propels youngsters to remain on track and locked in.

Chapter Two

How can parents support their child's interest in drawing?

Creative articulation through drawing isn't just a magnificent hobby for youngsters but additionally an essential instrument for their mental, close-to-home, and social turn of events. As guardians, sustaining and empowering this interest can encourage imagination, support certainty, and develop significant fundamental abilities. Here is an itemized investigation of how guardians can really uphold their youngster's energy for drawing.

Understanding the Child's Interest
Each kid is extraordinary, and their advantage in drawing might appear in different ways. A few kids normally float towards doodling or portraying, while others might show interest through narrating or inventive play. Noticing these signs and giving open doors to imaginative articulation is urgent in sustaining their energy for drawing.

Creating a Supportive Environment
To support and support their advantage, it's fundamental to make a devoted space where

they can uninhibitedly investigate their innovativeness. Setting up a workmanship corner with simple admittance to an assortment of craftsmanship supplies like: Paper, Pastels, Markers, paints, and Brushes can light their creative mind and inspire them to draw.

Encouraging Practice and Skill Development

Like any other skill, drawing requires practice and persistence to move along. Urge your youngster to draw consistently, whether it's a couple of moments every day or longer meetings at the end of the week. Offer encouraging feedback and helpful criticism to support their certainty and persuade them to keep refining their abilities.

Exploring Different Techniques and Styles

Open your kid to an extensive variety of drawing procedures, styles, and mediums to extend their creative skylines. Acquaint them with various instruments like charcoal, pastels, or advanced drawing cushions, and support trial and error with different surfaces and tones.

Celebrating Achievement

Showing your kid's fine art at home or in an assigned display space can approve their endeavors and urge them to invest heavily in their manifestations. Moreover, think about entering their work in neighborhood craftsmanship contests or displays to feature their ability and move further investigation.

Being a Role Model

Show others how it's done by participating in imaginative exercises close to your youngster. Whether it's doodling together in a sketchbook or leaving on workmanship projects as a family, sharing your own energy for craftsmanship can move and rouse them to seek after their inclinations with excitement.

Supporting Growth and Progression

Search out open doors for your youngster to additionally foster their drawing abilities, for example, by enlisting them in workmanship classes or studios custom-made to their age and interests. Urge them to look for direction from experienced specialists or coaches who can give important criticism and consolation.

Embracing Mistakes and Learning Opportunities

Urge your kid to investigate their creative mind through drawing by recommending prompts or subjects for their work of art. Support narrating through their drawings, permitting them to offer their viewpoints, sentiments, and thoughts in a visual configuration.

Balancing Support and Independence

Assist your kid with understanding that committing errors is a characteristic piece of the imaginative cycle and a chance for development and learning. Urge them to embrace blemishes and view them as open doors to analyze, learn, and move along.

Addressing Challenges and Frustrations

While it's vital to give direction and consolation, allow your kid the opportunity to freely investigate their imaginative advantages. Try not to force your own assumptions or guidelines, and on second thought, center around sustaining their interesting style and innovative voice.

Remaining Drew in and Involved

Keep a continuous discourse with your kid about their drawings, posing unconditional inquiries to start discussion and understanding their inventive strategy.

Encouraging Interdisciplinary Connections

Urge your kid to investigate how drawing can meet different subjects like science, history, or writing. Urge them to make drawings motivated by their inclinations and encounters, encouraging associations between various subject matters and innovativene

Chapter Three

At What Age Is Suitable to Introduce Drawing to Children?

Drawing is a principal type of articulation that holds massive worth in a youngster's turn of events. From cultivating imagination to upgrading mental abilities, the advantages of acquainting yourself with drawing with youngsters at an early age are tremendous and significant.

Early Childhood Development and Creativity

In the early stages of experience growing up, imagination assumes an essential part in forming a kid's viewpoint of the world. Presenting drawings at this stage energizes the creative mind and self-articulation, establishing the groundwork for imaginative reasoning further down the road.

Cognitive Development Through Drawing

Taking part in drawing exercises animates different mental capabilities, including critical thinking, spatial mindfulness, and scrupulousness. As kids control shapes and tones on paper, they foster decisive reasoning abilities and grow their psychological capacities.

Emotional Expression and Drawing

Drawing fills in as a strong source for close-to-home articulation, permitting youngsters to convey their sentiments and encounters in a protected and helpful way. Through workmanship, youngsters figure out how to recognize and deal with their feelings, cultivating the capacity to understand individuals on a profound level and demonstrating flexibility.

Motor Skills Development

The demonstration of holding a pencil and making blemishes on paper is instrumental in refining fine coordinated movements in small kids. Drawing reinforces dexterity and holds strength, laying the foundation for future exercises like composition and creation.

Social and Communication Skills

Drawing gives kids an all inclusive language through which to impart and interface with others. By sharing their work of art and teaming up on projects, kids foster interactive abilities like sharing, collaboration, and compassion.

Choosing the Right Age

Deciding the ideal age to acquaint drawing with youngsters relies upon different variables, including individual status, formative achievements, and parental direction. While there is nobody size-fits-all methodology, specialists propose that little children as youthful as a year and a half can profit from basic drawing exercises.

Acquainting Drawing with Little Children

For little children, the attention ought to be on investigation and tactile encounters. Giving enormous, simple to-hold colored pencils and offering amazing open doors for mark-production on various surfaces can ignite their interest and inventiveness.

Acquainting Drawing with Preschoolers

Preschoolers are anxious to explore and refine their abilities. Empowering them to draw unmistakable shapes, items, and individuals cultivates certainty and self-articulation. Basic prompts and narrating can motivate their creative mind and story abilities.

Making way for drawings

Establishing a steady climate that commends imagination is fundamental for supporting a kid's advantage in drawing. Assigning a committed craftsmanship space with open materials and showing youngsters' work of art can build up their deep satisfaction and achievement.

Parental Involvement and Support

Guardians assume a fundamental part in cultivating an adoration for craftsmanship in their youngsters. Empowering unassuming investigation, giving positive criticism, and partaking in drawing exercises together reinforce the parent-kid bond and impart a long-lasting appreciation for imagination.

Identifying Interest and Readiness

Noticing signs, for example, interest in jotting, interest with varieties, and ability to participate in workmanship related exercises, can assist guardians with checking their kid's preparation to begin drawing. Regarding every youngster's one-of-a-kind speed and preferences, is fundamental.

Empowering trial and error and play

Establishing a low-pressure climate where youngsters go ahead and trial and commit errors is critical for encouraging an uplifting outlook towards craftsmanship.

Defeating Difficulties

It's normal for youngsters to encounter disappointment and hair-splitting while participating in imaginative undertakings. Empowering a development outlook, stressing exertion over results, and approving their endeavors can assist youngsters with defeating snags and foster versatility.

Chapter Four

Drawing can be highly therapeutic for children dealing with emotions due to several reasons

Articulation of Feelings

Youngsters frequently find it trying to communicate their feelings verbally, particularly assuming that they're encountering intricate or overpowering sentiments. Drawing gives a non-verbal outlet for them to communicate what they're going through. They can utilize varieties, shapes, and images to convey their feelings, such that they feel great and safe.

Externalization of Feeling

When youngsters draw their feelings, they externalize them onto paper. This externalization can give a feeling of distance and viewpoint, permitting them to see their feelings from an alternate point. It can likewise assist them with understanding that their sentiments are discrete from themselves, which can be enabling and decreasing sensations of being overpowered.

Visualization and imaginary

Attracting permits kids to picture their feelings and encounters. By externalizing their sentiments through symbolism, they can acquire a superior comprehension of what they're going through. This interaction can assist them with getting a handle on their feelings and encounters, prompting expanded mindfulness and profound knowledge.

Sense of Control

Taking part in imaginative exercises like drawing provides youngsters with a feeling of command over their feelings. They can pick what to draw, how to draw it, and what tones to utilize, which can be enabling, particularly when they might feel weak notwithstanding their feelings.

Therapy and Delivery

Drawing can act as a therapeutic delivery for youngsters, permitting them to give out repressed feelings in a sound way. As they draw, they might encounter a positive feeling and gentility as they express and deliver what they've been holding inside.

Distraction and Relaxation

Participating in drawing can give a much needed diversion from overpowering feelings. Zeroing in on the inventive strategy can assist children with briefly moving their consideration away from their difficulties, giving them a truly necessary break, and advancing unwinding.

Communication and Connection

Correspondence are sending and getting data. It's the words we say, the messages we compose, and the verbal and non-verbal communication we use. Association is more profound. It's the sensation of being perceived and heard. It's the bond we make with others. Consider correspondence, the scaffold, and association as the solid groundwork that holds it up. You can communicate something specific across the scaffold, yet on the off chance that the establishment is frail, the association probably won't be there.

Here's the reason both are significant: Compelling correspondence constructs solid associations. Solid associations have correspondence more significant.

By zeroing in on both, we can construct more grounded connections, share thoughts all the more successfully, and make an additional positive and grasping world.

Workmanship can act as a type of correspondence for kids who battle to verbally put themselves out there. Through their drawings, they can speak with others, including guardians, educators, or advisors, about how they're feeling. This can encourage more noteworthy comprehension and sympathy, as well as fortify the youngster's association with individuals around them.

Generally speaking, drawing can be an incredible asset for helping youngsters explore and adapt to their feelings. Whether they're feeling miserable, furious, restless, or confounded, the demonstration of putting pencil to paper can furnish them with a helpful source for articulation, reflection, and mending.

Chapter Five

How can children overcome perfectionism in their artwork

Conquering hairsplitting in craftsmanship can be a critical stage in a kid's imaginative turn of events, cultivating inventiveness, certainty, and flexibility. Here are a few techniques to assist kids with handling compulsiveness:

Encourage experimentation

Instruct kids that craftsmanship is about investigation and self-articulation, not just about making an ideal final result. Urge them to attempt new strategies, materials, and styles without stressing over committing errors.

Focus on the process, not the product

Accentuate the worth of the innovative approach over the eventual outcome. Assist kids with understanding that each step they take in making their crafts is important and that errors are a fundamental piece of learning and development.

Praise effort and progress

Rather than zeroing in exclusively on the result, acclaim kids for their work, imagination, and eagerness to attempt new things. Commend their advancement and upgrades, as opposed to flawlessly.

Set realistic expectations

Assist kids with the understanding that it's OK not to be great and that committing errors is a characteristic piece of learning. Urge them to lay out reasonable objectives for their craftsmanship and to zero in on partaking in the process as opposed to taking a stab at flawlessness.

Educate flexibility

Assist kids in creating strength by showing them how to adapt to difficulties and difficulties in their craftsmanship. Urge them to issue addresses, gain from their missteps, and endure through hardships.

Provide constructive feedback

Offer productive input that spotlights unambiguous parts of the fine art instead of generally making decisions. Urge youngsters to consider their work and contemplate how they can improve without being excessively basic.

Create a supportive environment:

Encourage a strong and non-critical climate where kids feel open to putting themselves out there imaginatively. Urge them to share their contemplations, thoughts, and sentiments about their craftsmanship, unafraid of analysis.

Lead by example

Be a positive good example by embracing flaws in your own fine art and showing kids that committing errors is OK. Share accounts of your own imaginative battles and how you've beaten them.

Showing others how it's done is an initiative style where a pioneer goes about setting a good example for their group. They exemplify the ways of behaving, hardworking attitude, and values they anticipate from their adherents. Here are a few central issues about showing others how it's done:

constructs trust and regard: When a group sees their chief trying sincerely and holding themselves to similar principles, it fabricates trust and regard. Individuals are bound to follow a pioneer they respect and have confidence in.

Establishes the vibe: The pioneer's conduct establishes the general vibe for the group. Assuming the pioneer is lethargic or compromises, it will probably be reflected in the cooperation. Then again, a diligent and moral pioneer will move their group to take a stab at greatness.

Benefits groups: There are many advantages to showing others how it's done. It can assist with further developing camaraderie, efficiency, and, by and large, execution. It can likewise assist with making a more sure and cooperative workplace. Help other people: Go ahead and take care of business and assist with outing your colleagues when they need it.

Be positive and energetic: An uplifting outlook can be infectious. Your excitement for the task will come off in your group.

Advance self-sympathy

Help kids to be caring to themselves and to perceive that they truly deserve love and acknowledgment, no matter what their imaginative capacities. Urge them to rehearse self-empathy when they feel baffled or disheartened with their fine art.

By carrying out these systems, youngsters can figure out how to embrace their innovativeness, defeat hairsplitting, and foster a better relationship with their work of art.

Chapter Six

Getting Started with Simple Shapes.

Basic shapes are the structure blocks of any incredible youngsters' book representation. They offer an establishment for making drawing in characters, settings, and items that are simple for youthful personalities to get a handle on and interface with. This is a breakdown en route to get everything rolling with involving essential shapes in your youngsters' book:

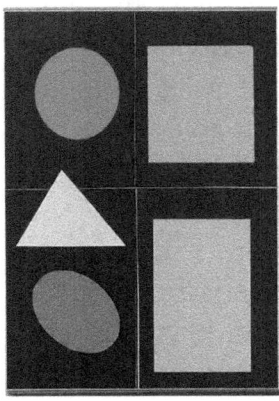

1. The Awesome Universe of Shapes:
Present the Stars: Begin by zeroing in on the most conspicuous shapes like circles, squares, triangles, rectangle, and ovals respectively as follows. Name and Play: Integrate the shapes' names into the story. Perhaps a circle is a blissful sun, a square is a comfortable house, a rectangle is an entrance door or a triangle is a cut of yummy pie.

Shape Chase: Energize collaboration by concealing shapes all through the outlines. Request that youngsters find the circles concealing in the mists or the triangles framing a mountain range.

2. Taking care of business Your Characters:
Building Blocks Approach: Consider each character a blend of straightforward shapes. A circle for the head, a square shape for the body, and more modest circles for eyes - a well disposed face is conceived.

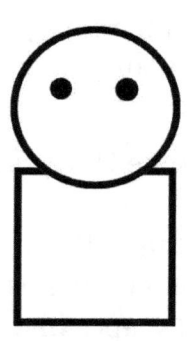

Character through Shapes: Use shapes to convey character. A tall square shape with sharp triangles for hair may be a naughty person, while a round circle with delicate bends could be a delicate companion.

Try not to overpower representations with such a large number of subtleties. Keep character shapes fundamental and permit kids to fill in the spaces with their creative mind.

3. Shapely Settings and Articles:
Natural Narrating: Use shapes to make the world your story happens in. A progression of wavy lines could be a moving sea, while

triangles stacked on top of one another could be a transcending tree.

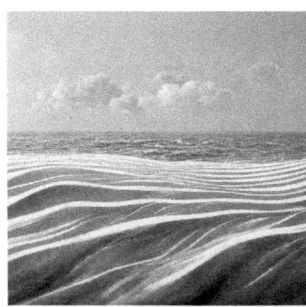 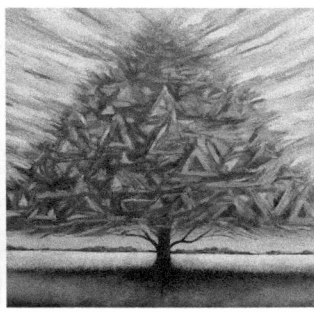

Shape Acknowledgment in real life: Let the shapes become ordinary items. A triangle with a line turns into a cut of pizza, and a square shape with a circle on top turns into a blissful bloom. Intelligent Components: Integrate straightforward shapes into pop-ups, folds, or other intuitive components to add an additional layer of commitment.

4. Past the Fundamentals:

Consolidating Shapes: As kids become familiar with fundamental shapes, acquaint them with mixes. A circle on top of a square turns into a snowman, and two triangles together structure a heart.

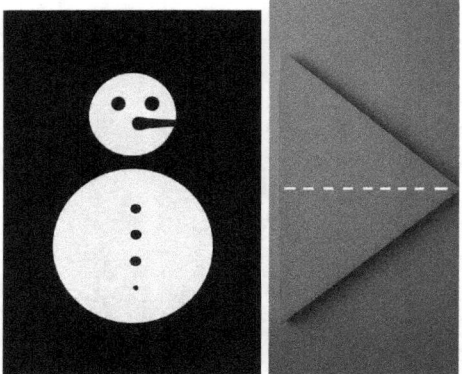

Playing with Size and Scale: Utilize the size and position of shapes to make profundity and viewpoint. An enormous circle somewhere far off turns into the moon, while a little triangle looking out from behind a square shape can be a modest creature.

Variety it Up: When the shape establishment is set, present brilliant, striking tones to rejuvenate your delineations.

The key is to keep it fun and looking in Allow the shapes to be a springboard for imagination, not a limit. With a perky methodology, you can utilize these principal building blocks to make an outwardly enthralling world in your kids.

Understanding Basic Shapes

Our general surroundings is loaded with astonishing shapes! From the round sun overhead to the square windows on a house, shapes are all over the place. Finding out about these essential structure blocks is a tomfoolery and significant stage for small kids. Here is a breakdown of a few normal shapes to kick your little ones off on their shape experience:

1. The Circle: Endlessly round We Go.

What it resembles: A circle is a totally round shape without any corners or closures. Envision a pizza, a ball, or a button - they're all circles.

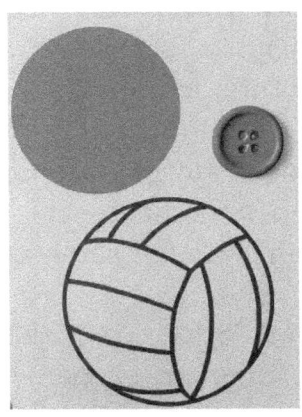

Picture of red circle, a yellow volley ball, and a blue button. Where could you whenever track down it? Search for circles in nature (sun, moon, ladybug spots) and ordinary items (wheels, plates, timekeepers).

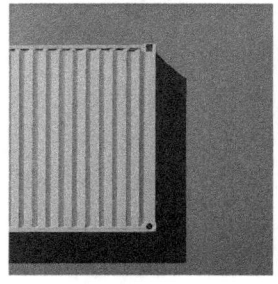

2. The Square: Corners In abundance
What it resembles: A square has four equivalent sides and four straight corners. Consider a crate, a window, or a napkin - all quite square.
Picture of green square, a cardboard box.
Where could you whenever anytime track down it? Squares are surrounding us in structures (entryways, windows), books, and, surprisingly, on cuts of bread.

3. The Triangle: Three's a Group (However Not really for Sides) What it resembles: A triangle has three straight sides and three corners. It can seem to be a cut of pie, a rooftop, or a traffic cone. Where could you at any point track down it? Triangles spring up in rooflines, cuts of watermelon, and, surprisingly, a few sorts of cheddar.

4. The Square shape: Long and Short, We Make a Match. What it resembles: A Square shape has four straight sides and four corners. It can seems to be a book, a case or a Television. Where could you at any point track down it? Consistently object like Television, box, telephone.

Tools and Materials Needed

The superb thing about drawing is that you needn't bother with a lot of extravagant stuff to get everything rolling. Here is an essential rundown of what you'll need to have close by for your youngster's imaginative undertakings Drawing Devices:

1. Pencils: Pencils are an incredible method for beginning since they're not difficult to delete in the event that errors are made. Get an assortment of pencil types:

2. HB Pencils: These are a decent universally handy pencil, not excessively hard and not excessively delicate.

3. 2H Pencils: These are more earnestly and really great for lighter lines and portraying.

B pencils: These are milder and great for more obscure lines and concealing.

3. Eraser: A decent quality eraser that eliminates pencil stamps neatly without smearing is significant.

4. Sharpener: Keep those pencils sharp for fresh lines!

5. Pastels: Colored pencils are an exemplary decision for youthful specialists and arrive in a large number of varieties.

6. Markers: Markers are another great choice, yet they can seep through paper so utilize a

thicker drawing paper if utilizing markers. Pick launderable markers for simple cleanup.
Drawing Paper:
7. Sketchbook: A sketchbook is an extraordinary method for holding all your youngster's drawings together. Look for one with heavyweight, corrosive free paper that will not seep through.
8. Drawing Paper: Customary printer paper will work, however heavyweight drawing paper is a superior choice as it can deal with deleting and different drawing materials without tearing.:
9. Hued Pencils: Shaded makes plans for come a huge range of varieties and take into consideration more point by point shading than pastels.
Sticks of charcoal or packed charcoal: These can be a good time for trying different things with various concealing methods. (Simply make certain, to have some child wipes available for cleanup!)
10. Oil Pastels: Oil pastels are a lively choice that makes an extraordinary surface on paper.
Rulers and stencils: These can be useful for youthful specialists who are simply beginning learning shapes and straight lines.

11. Planning Phase: A clipboard or cheap planning phase can give a solid surface to drawing.

Keep in mind: The main thing is to have a good time and trial! There are no incorrect ways of drawing, so urge your kid to allow their imagination to stream.

Top Tips for Amateur Doodlers

This book is for every one of the astounding Child out there who are simply beginning their undertakings in drawing! Prepare to transform your creative mind into pictures with these tomfoolery and simple tips:

1. Track down Your Apparatuses

Pencils are your companions! They come in various kinds, so you can explore different avenues regarding dull and light lines. Remember an eraser for those blissful errors. Pastels and markers let you fill your photos with brilliant tones. Use markers on thick paper to keep away from them seeping through. Paper is your material! A sketchbook is an extraordinary spot to keep every one of your manifestations.

2. We should Get Drawing

Begin with basic shapes. Circles, squares, and triangles are the structure blocks of all that you can draw. Lines get things going! Bended lines show development, while straight lines can make structures or fences.

Don't hesitate for even a moment to duplicate! See something you like in a book or magazine? Take a stab at drawing it yourself. It's an incredible method for learning new things.

3. Make it Brilliant

Variety outside the lines! In some cases the most astonishing pictures happen when you don't variety flawlessly.

Conceal it in! Utilize your pencil daintily at first to make shadows and make your drawings look 3D. Blend and match. Join pencils, pastels, and markers to see what tomfoolery impacts you can make.

4. Practice Gains ground

The more you draw, the better you'll get! Try not to get deterred on the off chance that your most memorable picture is more than a little flawed. Continue rehearsing and having a good time. *Draw all over! Convey a little scratch pad and pencil so you can catch your thoughts any place you go.*

Search for motivation! See nature, books, or even your most loved toys to track down things to draw.

5. Above all, Have Some good times

Drawing is tied in with articulating your thoughts! There's no set in stone manner to make it happen. Be senseless! Be innovative! Allow your creative mind to roam free and draw whatever fulfills you.

Flaunt your work! Balance your photos on the ice chest, give them to loved ones, or make your own craft show. Each extraordinary craftsman began as a novice. So snatch your devices, let your imagination stream, and prepare to turn into a doodling whiz.

Chapter Seven

Exploring Shapes and Structures

The world is loaded with astounding shapes and structures! From the roundness of a volley ball to the crisscross of lightning, these structure blocks are all over the place. We should jump into a great method for investigating shapes and structures in your drawings:

1. Shape Scrounger Chase: Get Outside (or Inside) Go for a stroll around your home, lawn, or neighborhood. Search for a wide range of shapes in your general surroundings. Spot circles in wheels, squares in windows, triangles in cuts of pizza.

Draw What You See: Back at home, snatch your paper and colored pencils. Draw the shapes you found! It very well may be a straightforward circle for the sun or a lot of triangles for a structure's rooftop.

2. Shape Recess: Shape March, Cut out various shapes from development paper. Circles, squares, triangles, stars - the conceivable outcomes are unfathomable! Allow your youngster to organize them on a piece of paper to make a goofy face, a senseless animal, or a delightful plan.

Shape Arrangement: Rather than cutting paper, utilize old magazines or papers. Allow your youngster to look for shapes inside the photos and cut them out. They can then make a remarkable collection utilizing these tracked down shapes.

3. Investigate Lines and Bends: Squiggle Time! Have some time off from sharp corners. Allow your kid to make free-streaming lines and bends on their paper. These can become moving slopes, a winding waterway, or the wavy tail of a cheerful canine Straight and Consistent: Spotlight on straight lines this time. Draw tall structures, long fences, or a bustling street with vehicles zooming by in *straight lines.*

Keep in mind: There are no off-base responses in craftsmanship! Urge your kid to explore, have some good times, and see their general surroundings in an entirely different manner: a world loaded with shapes and structures ready to be drawn. Drawing Circles and Ovals Circles and ovals are everywhere around us. Circles are entirely round, similar to a pizza or a ball. Ovals resemble crushed circles, a piece longer on one side. Next, we'll figure out how to draw these tomfoolery shapes.

Drawing Circles and Ovals

Hold your pencil: Grasp it tenderly, similar to when you're holding a pastel. Consider a ball, a button, or a plate. Move your arm, not your wrist: Keep your elbow on the table and move your entire arm to make a circle in the air. Practice in the air: Do a couple of circles in the air prior to putting your pencil on the paper. Daintily contact the paper: Begin at one spot and delicately move your pencil around, making a circle. You can definitely relax in the event that it's noticeably flawed. That is not a problem.

Attempt once more: Circles can be interesting. In the event that yours isn't round, eradicate it and attempt it once more. Careful discipline brings about promising results.

Reward Tip: Follow around with round objects Track down a cup, a top, or a coin and put it on your paper. Tenderly hold your pencil around the edge and follow the circle.

Oval Tomfoolery.

Consider an egg: Ovals resemble long circles, formed like an egg or a face. Begin with a circle: Draw a circle gently with your pencil.

Stretch it a piece: Imagine pulling the top and lower parts of the circle delicately to make it longer.

Draw on top and base: Daintily eradicate a little piece of the top and lower parts of your circle. Then, redraw a smooth line to interface the sides and make the oval shape.

Careful discipline brings about promising results! Very much like circles, ovals take a little practice. Sit back and relax in the event that yours is flawed right away. Continue on. Additional good times:

Might you, at any point, track down circles and ovals around your home? Search for plates, clocks, door handles, or even your face.

Whenever you've drawn a few circles and ovals, use them to make pictures. Draw a circle for a rabbit's head and ovals for its ears.

Keep in mind, the main thing is to have some good times and be imaginative.

Square and Rectangle

Prepare to turn into a form genius Today, we'll figure out how to draw squares and square shapes, two vital shapes.

Square Power.

Envision a container: A square resembles a completely level box with all sides a similar size.

Hold your pencil: Grasp it easily, similar to when you're holding a fork.

Make a straight line: Begin at one spot on your paper and define a straight boundary down, similar to a tall wall.

Pause and turn: When your line is as long as you maintain that one side of the square should be, pause and make a sharp turn to go right.

Another straight line: Define one more straight boundary across, very much like the first, yet all the same going right.

Turn once more: Make one more sharp go to go down. Interface the sides: Define a last straight boundary going up to meet the absolute first line you drew. This will finish your square! Yahoo! You've drawn a square.

Square shapes are fun. Square's cousin: A square shape resembles a square's crunched cousin, with sides that can be various lengths.

Begin with a line: Very much like with a square, define a straight boundary down as long as you maintain that one side of your square shape should be. Turn and go short: This time, rather than going as far as possible across the paper, make a sharp go to go right, however just for a more limited distance than the principal line. Another turn: Make one more sharp turn to go down. Interface the way back: Define a last straight boundary going up to meet the absolute first line you drew. This will finish your square shape. Analyze Take a stab at making square shapes with various side lengths. You can make them tall and thin or short and wide.

Reward Tip: Utilize a ruler to assist you with defining completely straight boundaries.

We should get innovative. Whenever you've drawn a few squares and square shapes, use them to make pictures. A square can be a window or a photo placement. A square shape can be an entryway or a vehicle. Might you, at any point, track down squares and square shapes around your home? Search for entryways, windows, books, or even a cut of bread.

Draw triangles and polygons:

Triangles are shapes with three straight sides and three corners. Envision a cut of pizza. That is a triangle.

The most effective method to draw a triangle: Get a pastel or pencil and make a dab anyplace on your paper. Imagine the dab as a yummy pizza hanging tight for a cover.

Without lifting your pastel, define a straight boundary down from the dab. Imagine you're drawing a yummy cut of pizza.

As yet, holding your pastel, define another straight boundary so it meets the main line you drew, making a sharp corner. Imagine you're drawing one more yummy cut close to the first

Lift your pastel and step in a straight line back to the speck where you began. Presently, you have a triangle Yippee, Your pizza cuts are finished and make a yummy triangle.

Polygons are shapes with many straight sides and corners. A triangle is likewise a sort of polygon So anything with multiple sides is a polygon.

Instructions to draw a polygon:

Get a pastel or pencil and make a dab anyplace on your paper. Imagine this dab is the beginning stage of a tomfoolery expedition

Without lifting your colored pencil, define a straight boundary to one more right on the paper. This will be your subsequent corner. Each line you move is a stage nearer to tracking down the secret fortune. Continue to define straight boundaries from one corner to another, making as many corners (sides) as you need. The more corners you draw, the better your fortune map becomes. At the point when you're content with the quantity of sides, define a straight boundary from your last corner as far as possible back to the absolute first speck you made. Presently you have a polygon. You tracked down the fortune Praise your astonishing polygon-formed treasure map. Reward: Have a go at involving various tones for your triangles and polygons: Might you at any point draw a triangle with generally a similar length sides? This is called a symmetrical triangle. What number of sides might your polygon at any point have? There are squares (4 sides), pentagons (5 sides), hexagons (6 sides), and some more! Permit your innovative brain to wander indiscriminately.

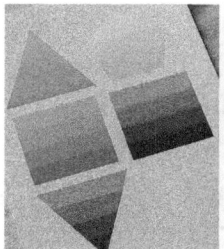 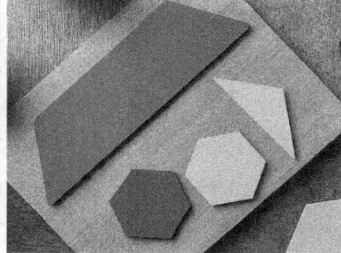

Chapter Eight

Transforming shape into object

There are two head approaches to deciphering "changing a shape into a thing"

Changing over a 2D shape into a 3D item: This cycle includes taking a level shape, similar to a square or circle, and giving it profundity and aspect to make a 3D portrayal. Here are a few normal methodologies:

Attracting viewpoint: This procedure utilizes disappearing focuses to make the deception of profundity on a level surface. By broadening the lines of your 2D shape towards evaporating focuses, you can make a fundamental 3D structure.

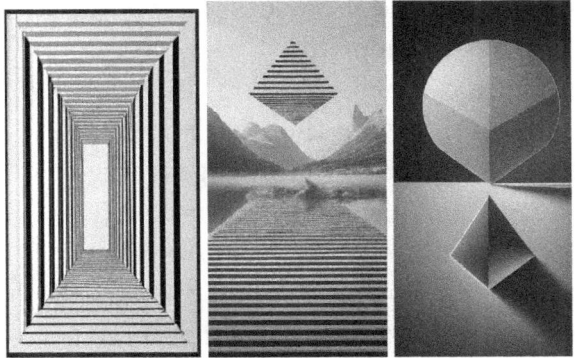

3D programming: Plan programs like Blender or Maya permit you to construct 3D articles without any preparation or by controlling existing shapes. You can expel a 2D shape to give it depth, or use it as a diagram to build a more perplexing 3D model.

Papercraft: Here, you make a 3D item by removing and collecting 2D shapes. This is an extraordinary, involved method for imagining the change from level shapes to 3D structures.

Changing over a computerized way into a strong item: In plan programming like Adobe Artist, a shape is many times characterized by a way, which is basically a line illustrating the shape. You can change this way into a strong item over completely to control it further. This is how it's done:

Stroke to protest: This choice fills the shape illustrated by the way, making a strong item with variety or surface. This permits you to apply impacts and alter devices that wouldn't deal with a basic blueprint.

The technique you pick relies on your motivation. In the event that you're outlining or rehearsing viewpoints, drawing strategies may be adequate. For making complex 3D models or controlling computerized craftsmanship, 3D programming or configuration apparatuses offer further developed choices.

Basic Object Drawing Exercises

Flash Innovativeness and perception abilities
Drawing is a fabulous way for youngsters to foster their innovativeness, dexterity, and perception abilities. Here are a few toys and simple activities that utilize essential shapes to acquaint them with drawing objects:

Practice 1: Shape Countenances
Materials: Paper, pencils, pastels, markers (anything they like to draw with)
Guidelines:
Begin by drawing a basic circle.
Ask your youngster, "What could this circle at any point be?" Contingent upon their age, they could say a sun, a ball, a button, or even a cheddar puff! Urge them to be inventive.
When they have a thought, assist them with adding subtleties with fundamental shapes. For instance, a bright face could have triangles for eyes and a bended line for a grin. A ball might have more modest circles drawn on for polka specks.
Allow them to add tone and some other subtleties that they like.

Practice 2: Line Houses
Materials: Paper, pencils, rulers (discretionary)
Directions:
Define a straight boundaries on the paper to address the essential design of a house.

You can do basic squares and square shapes, or even triangles for a more capricious house.

Guide your youngster to add subtleties utilizing more lines. A skewed line across the top can be the rooftop. Short lines descending from the rooftop can be drains. A square shape as an afterthought can be an entryway.

Allow them to add windows with squares or square shapes, a fireplace with a triangle on top, and perhaps a way prompting the entryway with a different line.

Urge them to variety their home and add subtleties like blossoms, trees, or a post box.

Practice 3: Circle Vehicles

Materials: Paper, pencils, pastels, markers

Guidelines:

Draw an enormous circle on the paper.

Inquire, "What might this circle at any point be?" This time, it very well may be a vehicle, a bike wheel, a doughnut, or even a controlling wheel.

On the off chance that it's a vehicle, assist them with adding subtleties with more modest circles for wheels (on the lower part of the large circle). Square shapes can be windows, and a more modest square shape on top can be the windshield.

Allow them to add subtleties like triangles for headlights, a bended line for a guard, or even a squiggly line on top for smoke emerging from a fume pipe (on the off chance that it's a cool *race vehicle*).

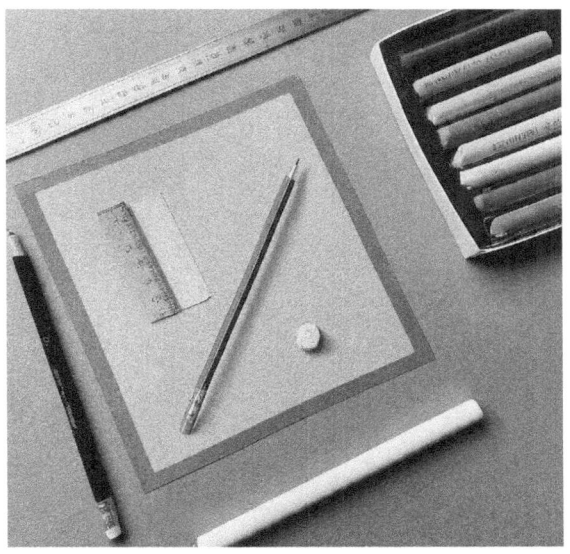

Keep in mind: Keep it basic, Begin with fundamental shapes like circles, squares, square shapes, and triangles.
center around the fun of making and investigating their creative mind.
Allow them to start to lead the pack and be innovative! There's no set-in-stone manner to draw these articles.
As they settle in, you can challenge them with somewhat more mind boggling shapes like ovals, pentagons, or even stars.

These are only a couple of thoughts to kick you off. There are vast opportunities for transforming essential shapes into fun and unmistakable articles. With a touch of support, your youngster will be shocked at what they can make.

Combining Shapes Creatively

Consolidating shapes is a key imaginative method used to make complicated and intriguing items, characters, and scenes. It's an integral asset for the children at the age of two and grown-ups to investigate their innovativeness and foster plan abilities. Here is a definite clarification on the most proficient method to get everything rolling:

Figuring out shapes:

Essential Shapes: Begin by getting to know the central structure blocks: circles, squares, square shapes, triangles, and varieties like ovals, pentagons, and bows.

Shape Properties: Investigate the attributes of each shape. Circles address completeness or development. Squares and square shapes recommend stability or construction. Triangles inspire activity or headings.

Joining Systems:

Covering: Layer shapes somewhat on top of one another to make a feeling of profundity and aspect. Imagine a circle for a head with a more modest square covering somewhat for the mouth.

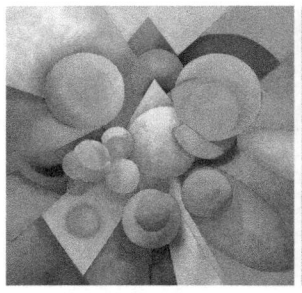 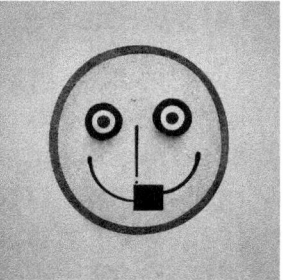

Interlocking: Fit shapes together flawlessly to frame a new, brought together item. Consider unique pieces where squares and triangles interface to make a bigger structure.

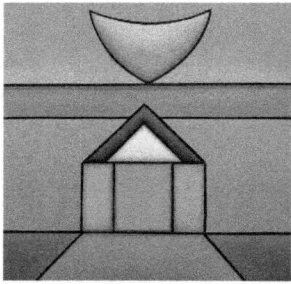 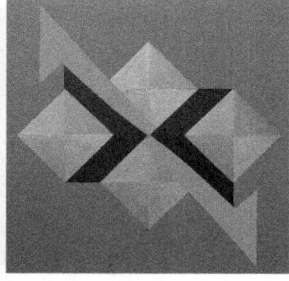

Deducting: Utilize negative space by removing states of different shapes. Envision a square with a roundabout pattern in the middle to turn into a doughnut.

Redundancy: Make examples or surfaces by rehashing a solitary shape or a blend in a particular plan. Consider lines of squares framing a block facade or triangles shaping scales on a fish.

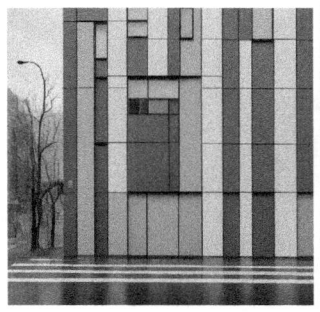 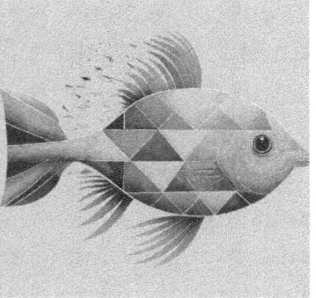

Improving Inventiveness:
Change: Use shapes as beginning stages and change them imaginatively. Stretch a circle to turn it into an oval for a body. Transform a square into a trapezoid for a skewed rooftop.

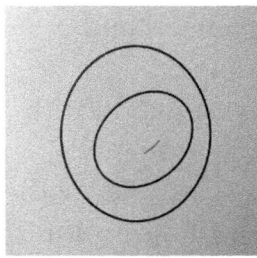 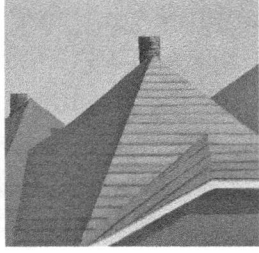

Point of View: Ponder how shapes show up from various points. A circle from the side turns into an oval. A square shifted on its corner turns into a jewel.

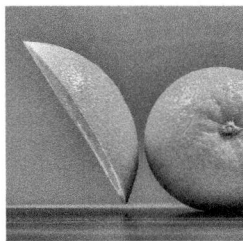 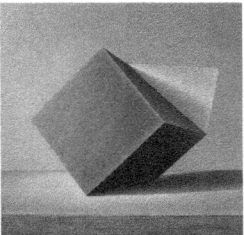

Reference: Check out certifiable items or pictures for motivation. How are normal structures derived from essential shapes? Could you at any point reproduce them utilizing your mixes?

Models and Exercises:

Creatures: Consolidate circles, ovals, triangles, and square shapes to make fun, loving creatures. Utilize a circle for the body, ovals for ears, and triangles for balances or bills.

Robots: Squares, square shapes, and triangles can frame the body, arms, and legs. Circles become eyes or wheels. Allow your creative mind to roam free with pinion wheels and contraptions produced using shapes.

Conceptual Craftsmanship: Investigation with covering and differentiating shapes to make outwardly captivating organizations. Play with varieties and examples to add profundity and interest.

Keep in mind: There are no severe standards! Embrace trial and error and see what startling blends arise. Careful discipline brings about promising results! The more you consolidate shapes, the more agreeable and certain you'll turn out to be. Utilize different mediums paper, pencils, paints, and computerized apparatuses to investigate different innovative potential outcomes.

Adding Depth and Perspective

Making Your Drawings Wake Up: Grasping Profundity and Point of View for Youngsters Have you at any point drawn an image and wished it looked all the more genuine, similar to you could hop directly into it? That is where profundity and viewpoint come in. They are superpowers that craftsmen use to cause their drawings to feel three-layered (3D), despite the fact that they are on a level piece of paper. Profundity is about how close or distant things appear to be in your drawing. Here are a few cool stunts to show profundity:

Size matters! Things nearer to you will look greater, and things farther away will look more modest. Envision a monster remaining close to a minimalistic home. the goliath is a lot nearer, so we draw it greater. Covering objects is another profundity stunt. On the off chance that you draw a tree behind a house, you just see part of the tree on the grounds that the house is in front. Have a go at concealing a portion of what you're attracting behind one more part to show it's farther away.

Subtleties, Things nearer to you will have more subtleties, similar to lines showing the bark on a tree. Distant things will not have as many subtleties; they may very well be a foggy shape.

View point resembles glancing through an enchanted window at your drawing. It assists in showing where things are dispersing, similar to how distant a street appears to go. Here is a straightforward method for mulling over everything:

Envision a train track loosening up before you. As the tracks move farther away, they appear to draw nearer together, similar to when they are meeting at a point somewhere far off. This point is known as the disappearing point. Whenever you draw streets, corridors, or train tracks, you can utilize evaporating focuses to make them appear as though they retreat into the distance.

Here is a great movement to attempt! Draw a scene like a street prompting a house. Make the street more modest as it goes towards the house (farther away) and draw the house greater in light of the fact that it's nearer. You might conceal part of the street behind the house to show it's in front.

Keep in mind, these are only a couple of ways to make your drawings seriously energizing! Make it a point to try and have a great time. The main thing is to be innovative and continue to draw.

Chapter Nine

Adding Details and Texture

We should make our drawing extra wonderful with subtleties and surfaces. Have you at any point drawn an image and felt like it was missing something special? That is where subtleties and surfaces come in. They're similar to the sprinkles on your frozen yogurt parfait; they make your craftsmanship much more flavorful (and fun!) to check out.

Subtleties are like minuscule zooming powers
What are subtleties? Subtleties are the easily overlooked details that make your drawing wake up. They can be things like:

Buttons on a shirt

Eyes and hairs on a feline

Blocks on a house

Leaves on a tree

How to add subtleties? Take a look at what you're drawing. What are the little things you see? Utilize your pastels, pencils, or markers to add those little subtleties to your image.

Surfaces resemble feeling your drawing.
What are surfaces? Surfaces are the manner in which things feel on a superficial level. They can be harsh, smooth, uneven, sparkling, or even fluffy.

How to add surfaces? You can't actually contact your drawing, yet you can show how things would feel by utilizing various lines, shapes, and varieties:

Harsh: Scrawl short, uneven lines to show an unpleasant stone.

Smooth: Utilize long, stunning lines to show a smooth, sparkling vehicle.

Uneven: Draw little circles or ovals near one another for a rough street.

Sparkly: Variety with light, gleaming shades to show something glossy.

Fluffy: Make little, squiggly lines near one another for something fluffy like a sheep.

We should rehearse.

Ponder an image you're now drawing, or you can draw another one. Here are a few plans to add subtleties and surfaces:

Creature: Add fur lines on a feline, scales on a fish, or quills on a bird.

Tree: Draw various shapes and sizes for the leaves. Utilize earthy colors for the harsh bark.

Blossom: Make the middle yellow and add lines for the delicate petals.

Keep in mind, there are no off-base responses The main thing is to have a great time and utilize your creative mind to make your work of art very cool.

Methods for adding subtleties

Transforming Your Doodle into a Work of Art: Detail Procedures for Youthful Specialists

At any point take a gander at your drawing and feel like something's absent. It may very well need a sprinkle of subtleties. Subtleties resemble the last little details on a superhuman ensemble: they make your fine art stick out and flaunt all your imagination.

Here are a few cool methods to add subtleties to your drawings that are really fun and simple for youthful specialists:

1. Turn into a detailed investigator.

Snatch your amplifying glass (or imagine one) and investigate what you're drawing. What little things do you see?

Creature: Are there fur lines on a feline, scales on a fish, or quills on a bird?

Bloom: Does the middle have an alternate tone? Are the petals smooth or unsettled?

House: Does it have windows with sheets? Are there blocks or siding?

2. We should talk lines: Lines are your closest companions with regards to subtleties. Utilize various sorts of lines to show various surfaces: Short, uneven lines: Harsh rocks, rough streets, the bark of a tree. Long, thrilling lines: Smooth, sparkling vehicles, streaming hair, the bends of a blossom petal. Wavy lines: grass, soft mists,

the wiggly body of a worm. Little dabs: Spots on a ladybug, spots on a face, stars overhead.

3. Concealing is super: Concealing with your pencil or pastel can add profundity and make your drawing look 3D. Hazier shades: Make shadows behind objects or under their bends. Lighter shades: Show regions where the light hits.

4. Design Power: Examples can add a tomfoolery and a fascinating touch to your drawings. Stripes on a zebra, polka spots on a ladybug, twirls on a shell. You might create your own examples.

5. We should get vivid: Make sure to explore different avenues regarding variety. Utilize various shades of a similar variety to add depth and surface. For instance, a green tree could have a few hazier green shadows and lighter green features.

Keep in mind:

There are no errors! In the event that you could do without how a detail looks, simply delete it and attempt again.

Careful discipline brings about promising results! The more you draw and add subtleties, the better you'll get at it.

Fun Shedding and Cross-Bringing Tips

Practice on circles and squares
Prior to drawing on your astonishing animal or article, take a stab at concealing and cross-bring forth on basic shapes to get its hang.

Make it a point to try: There's no set-in-stone method for concealing or cross-hatching. Mess about and see what cool impacts you can make. Utilize various pencils: Attempt a lighter pencil for delicate shadows and a hazier one for intense shadows.

Check genuine articles: Notice how light and shadows fall on your toys or even your hand out. This will assist you with concealing your drawings all the more, everything being equal.

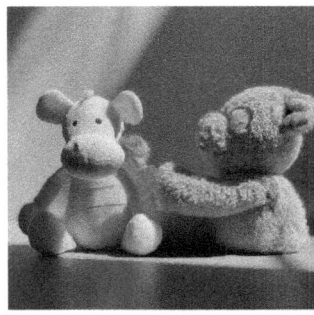 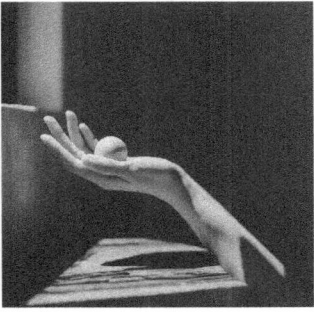

Keep in mind, concealing and cross-bring forth take practice, yet with a tad of

endeavoring, you'll make your drawings look phenomenal in a matter of seconds.

Chapter Ten

Understanding Proportions and Scale

Imagine a reality where seats are too enormous to even think about sitting on, or entryways are so little you need to slither through them. Our feeling of equilibrium and concordance in the visual world depends vigorously on two key ideas: scale and extent. While they are connected, they manage size in marginally various ways.

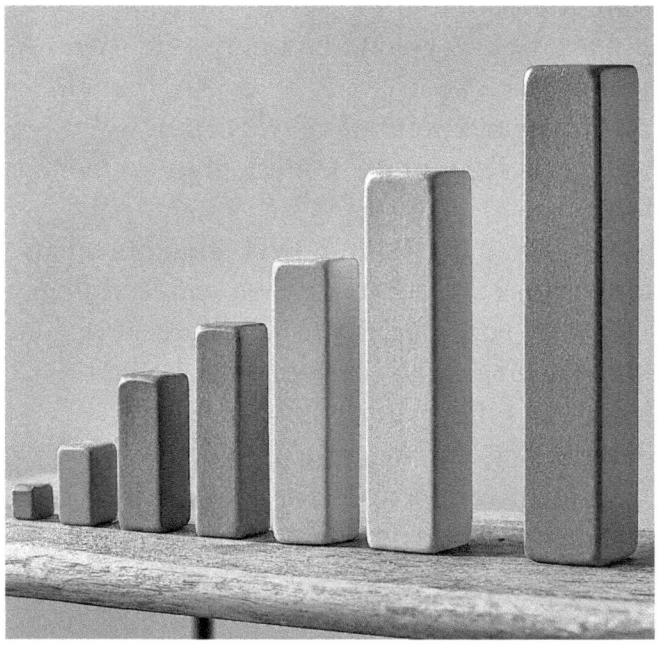

Scale: Evaluating the Scene

Scale alludes to the overall size of one item contrasted with another, or to a reference point. This reference point can be:

One more item in the scene: A goliath treat overshadowing a milk cup gives a feeling of caprice.

The actual craftsmanship: A scaled down house on an immense material causes the house to appear to be considerably more modest.

The Watcher: An entryway scaled for insects wouldn't be exceptionally easy to understand for people. By controlling scale, craftsmen and originators can make different impacts:

Accentuation: A goliath bloom in a field draws the eye.

Profundity and point of view: Distant mountains seem more modest, giving a feeling of distance.

Humor or dream: Overstated highlights on an animation character make them entertaining.

Extended: The Specialty of Equilibrium Inside Extent manages the connection between the pieces of a solitary item. It's tied in with guaranteeing the various components fit together outwardly and give a feeling of equilibrium. For example, in a human figure, the head ought not be greater than the middle.

Specialists have utilized different devices to accomplish this to a great extent:

The Brilliant Proportion: This numerical equation (generally 1:1.618) has been utilized for quite a long time to make satisfying organizations in craftsmanship and plan.

Perception: Concentrating on genuine articles and figures assists specialists with fostering an eye for normal extent.

Matrix Frameworks: Isolating a material into segments can support making adjusted extents.

The Force of the Pair:

Scale and extent cooperate to make outwardly fascinating and amicable theories. This is how it's done:

Scaling objects relatively: A goliath seat that keeps up with the right extents of an ordinary seat would, in any case, be unmistakable and feel like a seat, despite the fact that it's enormous.

Making contrast through scale: A minuscule vehicle close to an enormous truck underlines the size distinction of the vehicles.

By getting it and utilizing scale and extent really, craftsmen, planners, and, surprisingly, ordinary individuals can make outwardly engaging and effective works. Whether it's a painting, a structure, or, in any event, orchestrating furniture in a room, these ideas assume an imperative role in accomplishing a feeling of equilibrium and request.

Scales and Measuring Items Accurately

Grasping Scale and Estimating Articles
Scaling and measuring are principal ideas used to address and control the elements of an article. They are especially significant in different fields like designing, planning, map making (mapmaking), and, surprisingly, regular undertakings like creating or sewing.
Scale.

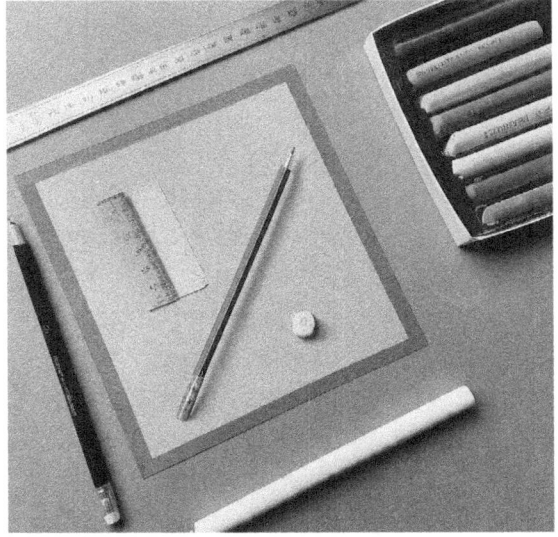

Scale alludes to the corresponding connection between the size of an item in a drawing, model, or picture (portrayal) and its genuine size in reality. It's communicated as a proportion, written in the organization "a:b."

This is the secret: a addresses the size of one unit in the portrayal (e.g., 1 centimeter on a guide). b addresses the size of the comparison unit in reality (e.g., 100 kilometers on the genuine ground). There are two well known ways of interpreting scale:

Bigger scope: A size of 1:10 implies that each unit in the portrayal relates to 10 units as a general rule. The portrayal is more modest than the genuine article.

More limited size: A size of 10:1 implies that each unit on the portrayal relates to 1/tenth of a unit as a general rule. The portrayal is bigger than the genuine article.

Measuring Items

Estimating alludes to the demonstration of changing the components of an item, either relatively (keeping up with the article's shape) or non-relatively (extending or crushing). Here is a breakdown of the two strategies:

Corresponding Measuring (Scaling): This includes keeping up with the first state of the item while changing its size. It's accomplished by increasing every one of the article's aspects (length, width, and level) by a similar element. This element can be a rate (e.g., expanding size by 200%) or a scale proportion (e.g., multiplying the size means a scale component of 2).

Non-Corresponding Estimating: This includes changing the item's aspects inconsistently, bringing about a mutilated shape. This may be positive in unambiguous circumstances, such as making a personification or stressing specific elements.

Picking the Right Methodology

The decision among scaling and non-relative estimating relies upon the specific situation: Scaling is favored when you really want a precise portrayal that keeps up with the item's unique extent. This is significant in specialized drawings, engineering models, and guides. Non-relative estimating is utilized for imaginative purposes, such as accentuation, or squeezing an item into a particular space.

Instances of Scale and Measuring

A plan of a house could utilize a size of 1:50. This implies that each 1 centimeter on the diagram addresses 50 centimeters (or a portion of a meter) of the real house.

A dollhouse is a downsized reproduction of a genuine house. It's an illustration of relative measuring, keeping up with the state of the house but at a more limited size.

An animation character with an enormous head and a little body is an illustration of non-relative measuring. The craftsman has misrepresented specific elements for imaginative impact.

By understanding scale and estimating strategies, you can successfully address and control objects in different settings, guaranteeing exactness or accomplishing an ideal imaginative impact.

Tips for Maintaining Proportions

Assisting messes around with dominating extent and size in their drawings is tied in with making craftsmanship tomfoolery and cultivating their creative certainty. Here are a few hints that make learning charming:

1. Perky Perception:

Reflect, Mirror on the Wall: Urge children to thoroughly search in the mirror and follow their hand or face. This assists them with understanding how various parts relate to size. Look into: Draw recognizable items next to each other, similar to a feline and a house. Discuss which is greater and why.

2. Shapes are our companions:

Straightforward Shapes Rule: Separate articles into essential shapes like circles, ovals, squares, and square shapes. This makes an establishment for building exact extents. Follow and Play: Let kids follow circles for heads, ovals for bodies, and lines for appendages. This assists them with picturing how shapes consolidate to make figures.

3. The Evaluating Game:

Measure With Fun: Use fingers, pencils, or patterns to quantify the size of various parts. For instance, an arm may be two head lengths long.

Envision and Draw: Request that children envision protests and examine their size relative to different things. Is a blossom greater than a butterfly?

4. Make it intelligent:

Drawing Games: Play speculating games where children draw something and others get it in light of its extent.

Duplicate Difficulties: Track down straightforward pictures in books or magazines and have children attempt to duplicate them, focusing on size connections.

5. Observe Imagination:

Try not to stress flawlessness: Remind kids that drawing is tied in with articulating their thoughts, not getting everything right.

Center around Progress: Appreciate how they might interpret extents over the long haul.

Reward Tip: Use drawing references! Take a gander at pictures of creatures, individuals, or items together and examine how the craftsman caught their size and extent.

Keep in mind, the key is to make it fun! By integrating these tips into fun loving exercises, children will foster areas of strength for drawing with exact extents and sizes, all while partaking in the innovative strategy.

Chapter Eleven

Mastering Lines and Curves

Building Blocks of Wonderful Drawings. Howdy, youthful specialists, Lines and bends are the superheroes of the drawing scene. They could appear to be basic, however together they can make anything you envision from wiggly worms to zooming spaceships. How about we separate the ways to dominate these cool apparatuses:

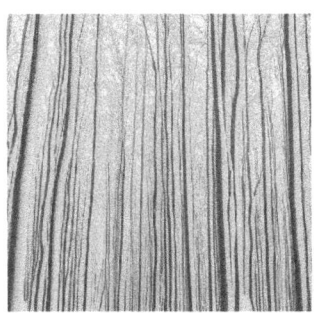

Line Up.
Straight Fighters: These lines go all over (vertical) or side to side (even). Envision a tall tree (vertical) and a drawn out, difficult experience (level).

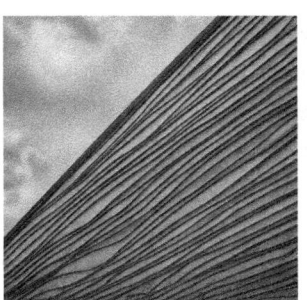

Incline Crew: These lines aren't frightened to shift. They can incline left or right, assisting us with drawing things like rooftops or tree limbs.

Freehand Companions: In some cases, lines just want to squirm. Freehand lines are for drawing anything that isn't entirely straight, similar to a wavy feline's tail.

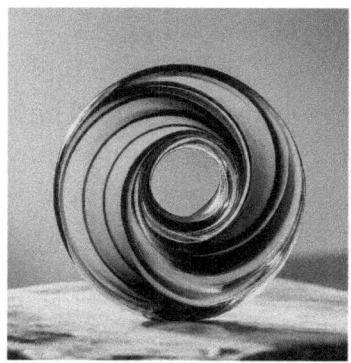

Breathtaking Team: Endless round: Circles are the bosses of bends, They're ideally suited for drawing suns, balls, or even a charming button nose.

All Over We Go: Bends can likewise resemble moving slopes. Take a stab at drawing a major "U" shape for a blissful grin or a more modest "U" for a rainbow.

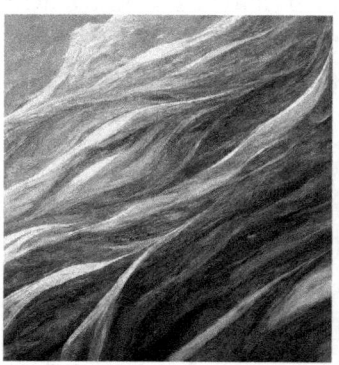

Squiggle Power: Very much like freehand lines, some of the time, bends love to squiggle and squirm. Use them for drawing anything fun and thrilling, similar to a

snake or a feathery cloud.
Careful discipline brings about promising results.Here is the tomfoolery part: practice! Snatch your paper and pencil, and how about we play:
Line Labyrinth: Draw a labyrinth with various types of lines - straight, skewed, and freehand. Check whether you can explore your direction without lifting your pencil.

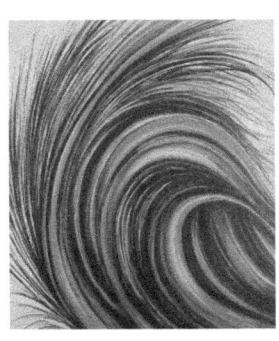

Bend Challenge: Draw a wide range of bends of all shapes and sizes, round and squiggly. Could you at any point interface them to make a senseless animal or a crazy bloom?
Glance Around, Draw Around: Track down motivation in reality. Take a gander at the lines and bends on your toys, furniture, or even your own body. Presently, attempt to draw them on paper.

Keep in mind, there are no errors in the drawing scene. In the event that your line is noticeably flawed, that is totally fine. It simply adds to your remarkable style. The main thing is to have some good times and continue to rehearse.

Reward Tip: When you become familiar with lines and bends, take a stab at consolidating them to draw a wide range of things! A straight line with a bend toward the end can be an entertaining nose. A circle with squiggly lines emerging from it tends to be a blissful sun. The potential outcomes are unfathomable.

Types of Lines and Curves and Their uses

The Structure Blocks of Your Drawings. Howdy, youthful craftsman, Lines and bends resemble the enchanted fixings that assist you with making anything you envision on paper. How about we investigate the various sorts and see what cool things we can draw with them.

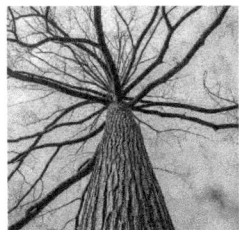

Straight Line Stars: Standing Tall: Envision a tree aiming high. That is an upward line, going straight and unpredictable.

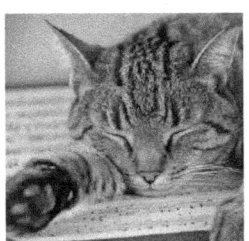

Dozing Excellence: Presently picture a feline sleeping. That is a level line, running across the page.

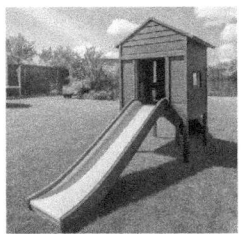

Incline Companions: Lines can likewise incline, similar to a slide at the jungle gym. These are askew lines, zooming all over but not exactly straight.

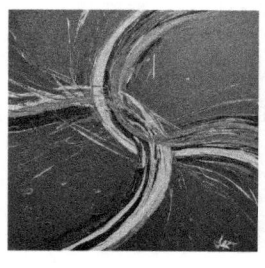

Crisscross Party: At any point, seen a lightning bolt? That is a crisscross line, b sharp turns that seem as though they're moving.

Surprising Champions:

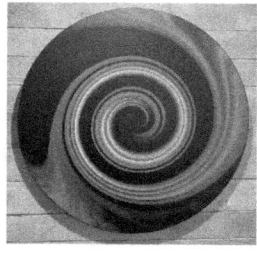

Endlessly round: Consider a ball bobbing. That smooth, round way it makes is a circle, an impeccably closed bend.

Grinning Wide: Presently envision a blissful sun. That bended line that twists upwards resembles a cheerful face.

Glare Town: Yet the sun is upset all of the time. A bend that twists downward resembles a grimace.

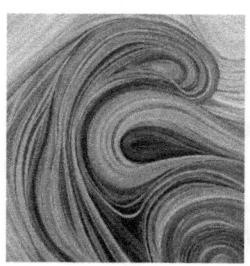

Squiggly Tomfoolery: Lines can squirm and wriggle as well. These are free-streaming bends, similar to a worm slithering or a wavy strand of hair.

Blending and Coordinating:
The genuine enchantment happens when you consolidate these lines and bends! Here are a few thoughts:
Straight lines can make a house (vertical walls and a skewed rooftop!), a wall (even pickets and vertical posts), or a teeter-totter (inclining radiates!).

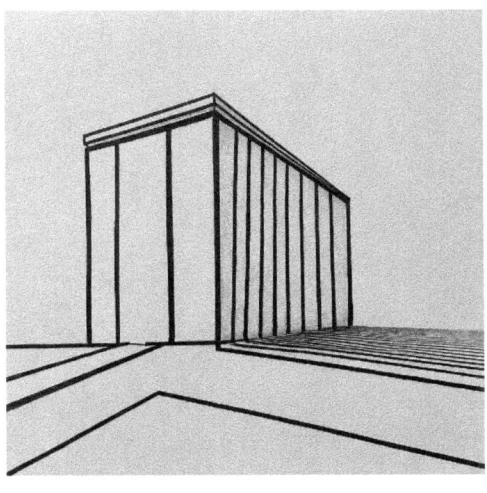

Surprising lines assist with drawing a bloom (round petals and a stunning stem), a snake (heaps of squiggly bends!), or a rainbow (a major, vivid circular segment). You could involve crisscross lines for lightning in a blustery sky or the sharp teeth of a crocodile.

Keep in mind: There are no incorrect ways of defining boundaries and bends. Try, have a great time, and see what astounding things you can make.

Drawing Curves and Contour

The Universe of Bends and Forms in Drawing. What are bends? Envision a slide at the jungle gym. It goes all over in a smooth, bendy way, not with sharp corners. That is a bend!

Action: Draw a slide Use pastels or markers to draw a major, blissful slide in a smooth, bended way.

Drawing bends: We should utilize our pencils like little vehicles following a surprising street. We would rather not pause and turn strongly.

Movement: Follow the slide, Hold your pencil softly and gradually follow the bended line of the slide you drew before. center around keeping the development smooth.

Searching for bends

Bends are all over, Could you at any point track down them on your number one toy vehicle, a grinning face, or even a rainbow.

Action: Bend Forager Chase Go on a scaled down adventure around the house. Could you, at any point, find five things with bends in them? Portray the bends you find (delicate, steep, uneven, and so forth).

Action: Blindfolded Shape Work with an accomplice. Have one individual hold a soft toy or toys while blindfolded. The other individual aides their hand, gradually following the layout of the article. Then switch jobs.

Searching for shapes

Forms resemble wizardry lines, which show us the state of things! Could you at any point track them down on a ball, a leaf, or even your own hand?

Movement: Form Drawing Challenge Pick an item, like a natural product, a cup, or a shoe. Look carefully and attempt to draw its form with smooth lines, zeroing in on the shape without agonizing over subtleties.

Careful discipline brings about promising results.

The more we draw bends and forms, the simpler it gets.

Movement: Free Drawing Time Put away some time for unconditional drawing. Urge your kid to work on attracting bends and shapes in their fine art. Allow them to draw entertaining beasts, senseless appearances, or anything their creative mind makes.

Show the code behind this outcome.

Rehearsing lines: variety, How about we play with lines? Lines are the structure blocks of all that we draw. Very much like the way that letters make words, lines meet up to make pictures. However, lines aren't all straight and exhausting; they can be good and bad, long and short, wiggly and straight. Today, we will investigate the great universe of line varieties.

Practice Line variation

More grounded drawings: Various lines assist with showing various things in your drawing. Thick lines make things look intense and solid, while slender lines can be sensitive and light. You can draw anything you envision with the right sort of line.

Better Control: The more you practice, the simpler it Will define the sort of boundaries you need.

We should get drawing.

Here are some pleasant ways of rehearsing lines:

Line tumbling: Take your pencil for a walk. Define a wide range of boundaries - straight all over the place, crisscrosses, circles made of minuscule lines, loopy lines that go high and low.

Line Families: Make an entire group of lines. Draw a tall, glad daddy line, a short and squiggly child line, and a few medium-sized lines that are perfect.

Line Doodling: Scrawl and doodle with various sorts of lines.

Line Games: Play spasm tac-toe or interface four, yet rather than utilizing X's and O's, define various boundaries for every player. Thick lines for one, meager lines for the other. Turn up the good times.

Brilliant Lines: Use pastels, markers, or different hued pencils to define your boundaries.

Finished Lines: Take a stab at defining boundaries on various surfaces. Perceive how lines look on sandpaper, felt, or even your own hand.

Line Stories: Utilize various lines to recount a story. Thick lines can show areas of strength, and some times, slight lines can show something tricky.

Keep in mind

The main thing is to have some good times. Try not to stress over making things awesome. Simply partake in the realm of lines and see where they take you.

Chapter Twelve

Exploring Colors and Pattern

The world is brimming with astonishing varieties, and drawing allows us to rejuvenate those tones Yet, there's something else about variety besides filling things in. Today, we're going on an undertaking to investigate the wizardry of varieties and examples.

Variety Festival.

Variety Criminal Investigators: Check out the room! Might you at any point find something red, something blue, and something green? Colors are all over the place, ready to be found in your drawings.

Blending Sorcery: Play with your paints or pastels! Combine various varieties as one to see what new tones you can make. Red and yellow make orange. Blue and yellow make green. The conceivable outcomes are unfathomable!

Variety Feelings: Tones can cause us to feel a wide range of things. Red could feel invigorating, while blue could feel quiet. What varieties encourage you, miserable, or senseless? Use them in your drawings to show how you feel. Designs are like tunes they rehash in a pleasant manner! How do we perceive how we can involve designs in our drawings:

Spot the Example: Check out your garments or a rug. Might you, at any point, track down any examples? Stripes, polka dabs, or perhaps squiggles that rehash?

Design Jungle gyms: Draw a few basic shapes like squares, circles, or triangles. Presently, variety them in with an example: -stripes in a single square, polka dabs in another.

Rainbow Examples: Draw a rainbow with stripes of the relative multitude of varieties you love, Presently, add an example to each variety stripe: polka specks on the red, crisscrosses on the orange. Designed Animals: Draw a senseless beast or a well disposed feline. Presently, give them fur or scales made of your 1 example.

Designed World: Draw a house, a tree, and a blossom. Utilize various examples to make every one unique: -blocks with stripes for the house, leaves with polka dabs for the tree, and petals with whirls for the blossom!

Keep in mind

There are no incorrect ways of utilizing tones and examples! Analyze, have a good time, and let your creative mind roam free! The universe of variety and example is sitting tight for you to investigate.

Basic Colour Mixing Technique for kids to know

The Astounding Universe of Variety! A Very Fun Aide for Little Specialists

Colors resemble enchantment in a container, and you hold the brush! Finding out about the variety hypothesis resembles learning a mystery code to make your drawings much more incredible. Here is a breakdown to kick you off:

Essential Tones:

Envision three extraordinary variety superheroes: red, yellow, and blue. These are called essential tones. You can't blend different varieties to make them; - they're the first!

Auxiliary Tones:

Presently for some blending fun! At the point when you consolidate two essential tones, you make a spic and span tone. Here is the mysterious recipe:

Red + Yellow = Orange
Red + Blue = Purple
Yellow + Blue = Green
Secondary Tone
Red + Yellow Orange
Yellow + Blue Green
Blue + Red Purple

Auxiliary tones resemble the offspring of the essential tones. Really slick, correct?

Blending Optional Varieties In any case, the good times don't stop there! We can blend auxiliary tones as well:

Blending orange and yellow can give us various shades of yellow-orange.

Blending green and blue can give us various shades of blue-green.

Blending purple and red can give us various shades of red-purple.

By blending various measures of each tone, we can make an entire assortment of new varieties!

Tertiary Tones: We could blend an optional variety with an essential tone to make a tertiary tone. There are a lot more of these, however, the following are a couple of models:

Blending Auxiliary and Essential Colors

Orange + Blue Teal

Green + Red Brown

Purple + Yellow Olive green

Keep in mind, there are no mix-ups in craftsmanship, just blissful mishaps!

Here are a few ways to blend tones:

Begin with modest quantities of paint or colored pencil right away.

Blend the tones gradually and cautiously. Monitor which colors you blended to make another one. Above all, have a great time and be imaginative, Blissful blending.

Incorporating Pattern into drawing

Uncovering the Sorcery of Examples in Children's Drawings. Designs resemble building blocks for inventive articulation. They can change a basic bringing into a dazzling world, and consolidating them is a great way for youngsters to foster their creative abilities. Here is a breakdown to kick you off.

Beginning Straightforward: Simple makes it happen, Start with key examples like stripes, polka spots, or matrices. Allow your kid to define straight boundaries for stripes or use circle stencils for polka spots. Lattices can be made with squares or triangles. These essential examples are an incredible springboard for building certainty.

Shape Power: Make it a stride further by utilizing recognizable shapes like circles, squares, and triangles to make designs. Children can substitute shapes with straight lines, make a slanting line, or even make a bloom involving these shapes as petals.

Tracking down motivation:

Nature's Range: Glance Around! Blossoms, leaves, creature scales, and even snowflakes all have exceptional examples. Go for a stroll in the recreation area and notice the dull plans tracked down in nature. Urge your kid to reproduce these examples in their drawings. Our general surroundings, structures, textures, and regular articles frequently have fascinating examples. Paisley swirls, checkered floors, or the stripes on a most loved shirt can all be wellsprings of motivation.

Taking it up a score:

Rehashing the Good Times: When your kid is OK with fundamental examples, urge them to rehash a solitary example component all through their drawing. This could be a blossom shape rehashed to make a sprouting bloom bed or a wave design used to represent the sea.

Stirring it Up: As their abilities create, challenge them to join various examples. For example, they could make a striped foundation with spotted blossoms!

Keep in mind:

Keep it fun: The main thing is for your kid to partake simultaneously. Allow them to try, commit errors, and release their inventiveness.

Process Over Flawlessness: Spotlight on the delight of making designs instead of accomplishing an ideal outcome.

Investigate Various Apparatuses: Use pastels, markers, paints, stencils, or even patterns from development paper to make designs.

Chapter Thirteen

Experimenting with Different Styles

Getting Out of Your Usual Range of Familiarity: Trying Different Things With Various Styles

Trying different things with various styles is a critical piece of inventive development. It's tied in with pushing your limits, investigating new strategies, and finding what impacts you. Whether you're an essayist, a painter, a performer, or somebody who appreciates design, venturing outside your usual range of familiarity can prompt invigorating.

leapforwards and assist you with refining your own interesting voice.

Why Trial?

There are many advantages to be acquired from investigating various styles.

Find additional opportunities: By attempting new things, you open yourself up to a more extensive scope of inventive thoughts and methods. You could coincidentally find a strategy that turns into a foundation for your future work. Forward leaps: Trial and error can assist you with defeating imaginative road obstructions. At the point when you're trapped in a hopeless cycle, having a go at something else entirely can start new motivation and assist you with moving toward your work according to a new viewpoint.

Foster your abilities: As you try different things with various styles, you'll acquire new abilities and sharpen your current ones, This will make you more flexible and balanced.

Track down your own voice: Through trial and error, you can acquire a superior comprehension of what you like and dislike. This self-disclosure process is fundamental for fostering your own one of a kind style.

Step-by-step instructions to investigate.

Here are a few hints on the most proficient method to begin with testing:

Distinguish styles you appreciate: Take a gander at works by specialists you respect in various styles. What parts of their work do you see as intriguing? Attempt to integrate a portion of these components into your own work.

Set little difficulties: Don't attempt to update your whole innovative strategy short-term. Begin by setting yourself little difficulties. For instance, an essayist could have a go at composing a sonnet in a particular structure, or a painter could try different things with another variety range.

Embrace the unforeseen: Don't hesitate for even a moment to commit errors. Trial and error is tied in with attempting new things and seeing what occurs. Once in a while, the most joyful mishaps can prompt your most imaginative forward leaps. Look for motivation from outside your field: Search for motivation in other imaginative disciplines. A performer may be roused by a painting, or an essayist could track down motivation in a piece of engineering.

Get input: Offer your exploratory work to others and get their criticism. This can assist you with rethinking your work and recognizing regions for development.

Trial and error versus center

While trial and error is significant, finding an offset with centered practice is likewise essential. You would rather not be continually hopping, starting with one style and then onto the next, while never fostering your abilities in any one region. Consider committing explicit periods to trial and error followed by times where you center around refining a specific style or procedure. Embrace the excursion of trial and error! It's a tomfoolery.

Cartooning for Beginners

We should get cartooning! A Fledgling's Aide for Youngsters.

Welcome to the astonishing universe of cartooning! Here, you can make a wide range of interesting, cool, and strange characters. It's really fun and simple to learn. So snatch your 1 drawing instrument and prepare to release your inventiveness.

What you'll require:

Paper: Any sort of paper will work, yet printer paper or a sketchbook is perfect.

Pencils: A normal pencil for drawing and a hazier one for illustrating (discretionary).

Pastels, markers, or shaded pencils: To rejuvenate your kid's shows!

Eraser: For those cheerful slip-ups (in light of the fact that errors can assist us with learning).

Stage 1: Shapes are your companions!

Visual artists don't necessarily draw very sensible figures. All things considered, they utilize straightforward shapes to fabricate their characters. These shapes can be circles, ovals, squares, square shapes, and triangles.

Heads: Most animation heads are circles or ovals.

Bodies: These can be ovals, squares, or square shapes. Ponder what sort of body suits your personality. Is it tall and thin or short and round?

Appendages: Arms and legs can be lines or ovals associated with more modest lines for hands and feet.

Stage 2: We should construct a face.

Since you have a good head shape, now is the ideal time to add a few highlights.

Eyes: Cartoony eyes are normally large and expressive. They can be circles, ovals, or even squares.

Nose: Cartoony noses can be truly basic: a little triangle, a spot, or even a line.

Mouth: Is your personality blissful? Draw a major grin! Is it miserable? Perhaps a glare Investigate and see what feelings you can form.

Stage 3: Remember the subtleties!

When you have the fundamental face, add subtleties to make your personality interesting.

Hair: Spiky, wavy, straight; there are no guidelines!

Ears: Large, floppy, or small? what sort of ears does your personality have?

Garments: Give your personality a cool outfit or night wear, whatever suits their character!

Stage 4: Activity time.

What's happening with your personality? Is it running, hopping, or perhaps waving hi? Utilize your attracting to show their activity.

Stage 5: Variety Blast!
Presently comes the tomfoolery part shading! Utilize brilliant, striking tones to make your animation pop. You can likewise utilize various shades of a similar variety to add profundity.
Reward Tip: Careful discipline brings about promising results!
The more you draw, the better you'll turn out. Don't hesitate for even a moment to trial and attempt new things. There are no missteps in cartooning, just blissful mishaps!
Here are a few extra assets to assist you in your cartooning and venturing:
Keep in mind, cartooning is tied into having some good times and allowing your creative mind to roam free! So get your pencils and get making

Reasonable Drawing Strategies
Totally, reasonable drawing is tied in with catching the deception of a three-layered world on a level surface. Here is a breakdown of a few critical strategies to accomplish that:
Planning is critical.
Reference Matters: Having a great reference picture is essential. A decent reference ought to be sufficiently bright and catch the subtleties you need to depict. Consider utilizing highly contrasting adaptations of your reference to zero in on esteem scales (light and shadow).

Pick the Right Devices: While you can begin with fundamental pencils, putting resources into various grades (HB, 2B, 6B, and so on) considers a more extensive scope of values. Mixing apparatuses like tortillons or mixing stumps assist with making smooth advances.

Establishing the groundwork:

Creation is above all else: contemplate how you need to organize your subject inside the edge. Use strategies like the standard of thirds to make a fair organization.

Begin light: Start with a light sketch to lay out the fundamental Shapes and extents of your subject. Try not to stress over amazing lines; center around exactness.

Catching Light and Shadow: Esteem ScalesTrain your eye to see the various qualities (delicacy or murkiness) in your reference. A decent worth scale will go from exceptionally light to extremely dim with a full scope of mid in the middle between.

Concealing Methods: There are different concealing strategies, such as bringing forth, cross-incubating, and texturing. Attempt it and find what works for you.. Keep in mind, concealing is tied in with making smooth advances, so plan to successfully mix your strokes.

Building Authenticity:

Thinking in Shapes: Rather than illustrating everything, center around building structure through apparent shapes. This gives a more regular, three-layered look.

The Force of Edges: Not all edges are made equal. Sharp edges characterize the forefront, while gentler edges make profundity as articles subside out of the spotlight.

Subtleties Rejuvenate it: When you have the essential design, add inconspicuous subtleties like surfaces, hair strokes, or kinks. These subtleties revive your drawing.

Careful discipline brings about promising results:

Train Your Eye: Focus on how light associates with your subject, in actuality. This will assist you with making an interpretation of those perceptions in your drawings.

Make it a point to examine: Reasonable drawing is an excursion, so don't get deterred on the off chance that your underlying endeavors are flawed. Continue rehearsing and investigating various procedures to track down your imaginative voice.

Keep in mind, there's no one size-fits-all way to deal with practical drawing. With commitment and these strategies as an aide, you'll be well headed toward making incredibly detailed drawings.

Realistic Drawing Techniques

How about we Get Squiggly: Theoretical and Strange for Youngsters Customary pictures show things we find in reality, yet unique and strange workmanship are like jungle gyms for our minds. This is the way to transform your drawings into strange and superb masterpieces:

Dynamic Tomfoolery:

Shapes Rule: Circles, squares, squiggles, and masses: everything goes, Fill your paper with a wide range of shapes and sizes in various varieties.

Variety Disarray: Try not to stress over shading things how they "ought to" look. Make a Purple Feline with a Green Tail. Try different things with brilliant, intense tones, or attempt delicate pastels for a fantastic vibe.

Lines Lead the Way: Define boundaries that go all over the place: crisscrosses, straight lines, stunning lines. They can be thick, slim, or somewhere in the middle. See where the lines take you.

Dreamlike Antics:

Blend and match: Envision a butterfly with a fish tail or a tree with a house for leaves. Allow your most stunning plans to show some major signs of life.

Softening Frenzy: Draw recognizable things like clocks or faces, yet make them all melty and drippy. Is it true or not that they are dissolving in the sun? From nonsensicalness? It really depends on you how you draw it.

Monster and Small: Make a minimalistic home on the rear of a monster ladybug, or a feline pursuing a high rise mouse! Play with size for an astounding turn.

Tips for Awesome Workmanship

Make it a point to take an examination! There are no slip-ups in the unique and strange craftsmanship. The more insane, the better Utilize Every one of Your Provisions! Pastels, markers, paints, sparkle anything goes.

Have a great time. This is tied into allowing your creative mind to take off and partaking all the while.

Here are a few additional plans to ignite your innovativeness: Draw a scene with a sky loaded with stars and hearts. Make an animal with wings made of leaves. Plan a machine that makes bliss downpour.

Keep in mind, there's no set-in-stone method for doing digest or strange craftsmanship. So snatch your provisions and prepare to make something thoroughly unbelievable.

Chapter Fourteen

Fostering your own style for youngsters' drawing

Fostering your own imaginative style is a tomfoolery experience! Everything really revolves around taking what you love to draw and adding your own unique touch. Here are a few hints to kick you off en route to turning into a hotshot sketcher:

1. Investigate Various Things to Draw:

Creatures: Take a stab at drawing your number one pet or envision fantastical animals with rainbow scales or feathery wings!

Individuals: Draw your family, companions, or characters from your 1 stories. Perhaps they're wearing odd outfits or have insane haircuts!

Places: Draw your fantasy house, a mysterious woods, or the submerged world. Allow your creative mind to roam free!

2. Explore different avenues regarding shapes and lines:

Fundamental shapes: Circles, squares, and triangles can be changed into anything! A circle with a triangle on top turns into a cap, or a square with squiggly lines turns into a beast.

Thicker and more slender lines: Utilize thick lines for striking frameworks and slim lines for subtleties like bristles or fur.

Thrilling and straight lines: Play with lines that twist and squirm or lines that go straight and unpredictable.

3. Flavor it up with tones and examples:

Variety blasts: Utilize brilliant, striking tones or make a delicate and fantastic state of mind with pastels.

Blend and Match: Feel free to explore different avenues regarding colors that probably won't appear to go together. You could make something astonishing!

Designs in abundance: stripes, polka specks, crisscrosses designs add character to your drawings.

4. Take a gander at Different Specialists (yet don't duplicate):

Books and magazines: Take a gander at how different specialists use shapes, lines, and tones. What do you like about their style?

Exhibition halls (on the off chance that you can): Works of art and figures can rouse you with groundbreaking thoughts and methods. Keep in mind, your craft is one of a kind! Take motivation from others, however, don't duplicate it precisely.

5. Practice gains ground:

The more you draw, the better you'll get! Relax in the event that your most memorable drawings are flawed. Continue rehearsing and having a great time.

Draw consistently, regardless of whether it's only for a brief period.

Don't hold back at all to commit blunders! At times, the best drawings come from merry setbacks.

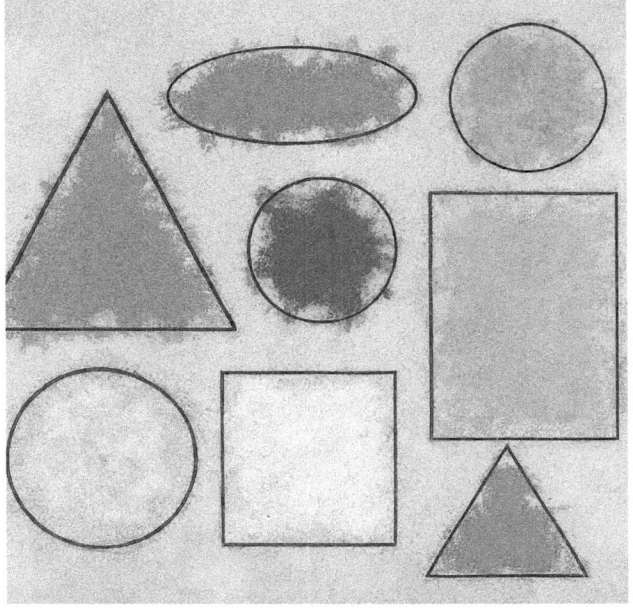

Reward Tip: Give your drawings senseless names. This adds to the tomfoolery and assists you with recalling your manifestations.

The main thing is to live it up! There are no errors in craftsmanship, so let your imagination stream and continue to attract your direction to your own amazing style.

Finding Motivation for Kids Drawing

Starting Imagination: Tracking Down Motivation for Youngsters' Drawings

Heard a young person say, "I don't have even the remotest clue what to draw!" It resolves this way in some cases, tragically, between young and old. However, stress not, there are lots of ways to kick off that creative mind and get those colored pencils going! Here is a tool kit loaded up with thoughts to move your little craftsman:

1. Glance Around

The world is overflowing with motivation. Go for a stroll outside and draw what you see: birds in the trees, entertaining molded mists, or a perky pup on a chain. Check out regular items in another manner. Is that seat a cantankerous beast or a cordial monster? Urge children to utilize their faculties. What sounds do they hear? What surface do they feel?

2. Storytime motivation

Books are entryways into astounding universes. In the wake of perusing a story together, have your youngster draw their number one scene, a person, or even their own conclusion This is an incredible method for joining perusing cognizance with creative articulation.

3. Allow music to play.
Put on certain tunes and let the music flash with inventiveness. Perky music could move a drawing of a moving creature, while more quiet tones could prompt a tranquil scene.

4. Make it a game
Games are a great method for getting those inventive energies pumping. Play "phone Pictionary," where you murmur an attracting thought to your kid, and they draw it. Then, the following individual thinks about what it is and murmurs a novel thought, etc

5. Craftsmanship challenge time
There are endless drawing prompts and difficulties on the Web and in action books. Attempt a "draw a beast with 7 legs" challenge or a "plan a hero ensemble" brief. These flash groundbreaking thoughts and assist jokes with investigating various ideas.

6. Check out different specialists.
Go on an outing to a gallery or peruse online craftsmanship exhibitions (with management, obviously!). Seeing items crafted by different craftsmen, both renowned and from their own networks, can move children to attempt new strategies or styles.

7. Embrace Missteps
We should jettison just a little! Empower trial and error and the possibility that "botches" can become something cool and surprising. A scrawl can transform into a beast's tail, or a wanderer's line can turn into a winding way.

8. The Force of the Creative Mind
Once in a while, the best motivation comes from just allowing the creative mind to roam free! Ask your youngster, "What might occur on the off chance that felines could fly?" or "What does the world resemble on the rear of a monster turtle?" Let their responses guide their drawings.

Keep in mind, the main thing is to have some good times! Strong support and a casual air will make your kid want more and more inventive undertakings.

See the furthest down the line updates to the Gemini Applications Security Hub. Opens in another window.

Conclusion

This book help to guide children on how to do drawing step by step, help them to learn about different shapes, how to become and excellent Artist.

www.ingramcontent.com/pod-product-compliance
Lightning Source LLC
Chambersburg PA
CBHW050316230526
45471CB00005B/2208